# WRITING PROMPTS
# FOR KiDS

Published by Monkey Publishing
Edited by Emily Hutchinson
Design by Paulo Duelli
Printed by Amazon


1st Edition, published in 2022
© 2022 by Monkey Publishing
Rheinstr. 9
12159 Berlin
Germany

ISBN: 9798404233162

# CONTENTS

## Chapter 1

## Chapter 2

## Chapter 3

## Chapter 4

# Chapter

# Unleashing the POWERS of this Book!

By reading this first page, you're setting off on a journey, an adventure into your own imagination with a fantastic end result, a story of your very own! As you work through the book you'll learn how to reach into your mind and pull out all those ideas that are hiding in there. You'll begin to put your ideas down on paper and create entire new worlds, amazing characters and action packed adventures. You'll learn how to revise and edit your story to make it even better, and add the finishing touches to make your story into a real book.

> "There is something delicious about writing the first words of a story. You never quite know where they'll take you."
>
> -Beatrix Potter (author & illustrator)

Within this book you'll find a wealth of story starters to give you a head to start to creating a story. With 40 starters to choose from, you're bound to find plenty that fires your imagination and inspires you to write. Each story starter sets you off with the beginnings of story, with a series of questions to help you to take that story further, develop it, and create a fantastic ending. We also give you exercises to help you with your stories and top tips for some extra hints to becoming a great writer.

How you use this book is up to you. You can work your way through, read the tips and have a go at the exercises in each chapter, or if you're really keen to get started, you can simply pick out a story starter that sounds interesting to you, and get writing! You'll get a lot out of reading the whole book and working through the exercises, but the story starters are always there for you, to dip into any time. Pick any story starter and let your imagination run loose. What will happen next? What places and characters will you add into the story? What adventures will there be along the way and ultimately, how will the story end? Happily ever after? Or something entirely different? These are all your stories, your worlds, and so it's all down to you to decide!

"I just write what I wanted to write. I write what amuses me. It's totally for myself. I never in my wildest dreams expected this popularity."

- J.K Rowling (author)

So whether you're carefully working through the exercises one by one, or diving straight in to the story starters, we hope you'll learn lots about story writing, become more creative and have a lot of fun that will spur you on to become a real author.

What are you waiting for? **Read on...**

# Story Starters
## 1 - 10

# Story Starter 1

The school science fair was approaching, and Polly couldn't wait to present her latest project. She was sure she would win first prize and leave everyone in awe. After all, you don't see a kid-made robot every day.

What was the robot able to do?

How did Polly come up with this idea?

Did Polly win?

# Story Starter 2

I knew I shouldn't have taken the short-cut through the woods. My parents had told me not to but it was late, I was tired, and there was a storm on the way. But when I saw the creature, I knew I'd made a really bad decision.

What did the
creature look like?

Why do you think the
creature was in the
woods?

Did I ever managed
to get back home?

# Story Starter 3

My dad had asked me to collect some sticks to start the fire while he set up the tent. Five minutes into my search I froze. Right there in front of me was a grizzly bear. I tried to remember what the park ranger had said. Play dead? Wave my hands? Run?

How did I feel?

What choice did
I make?

Was it really a bear?
Or could it had been
something else?

# ✦ Story Starter 4

Piper needed to take
a break from her
annoying little sister,
so she decided to hide
in the basement. She
settled on an old
sofa and opened her
book. But she soon
had a feeling she was
being watched.

Who was watching her?

Did the watcher show themselves or say something?

Was it friendly? Did it needed something from Piper?

# ✨ Story Starter 5 ✨

Robbie gasped in horror at the terrarium. He didn't know what had happened, but the lid had been moved and Pipi, his rainbow boa snake was gone. He started rummaging frantically through the room, but Pipi was nowhere to be found.

Where did Robbie look first?

Did he find Pipi?

Did Pipi encounter someone else in the meantime? How did they react?

# Story Starter 6

As soon as I drank a spoonful of the Smartness potion, I knew something had gone wrong. Suddenly my ears started itching and when I rushed to the mirror, I discovered that my face had gone green, my nose had grown three times its normal size, my hair had turned purple, and a horn was growing on my forehead.

Did I get help? If so, from whom?

Did I become super smart? Did the weird effects wear off? Or did I find a cure?

Did I see anyone and what was their reaction to my strange new looks?

# Story Starter 7

"JUMP JUMP JUMP" my classmates cheered me on. I had been standing still on the diving board for the last 10 minutes, unable to move in any direction. All I could see was how far away the pool seemed and how small the people on the ground looked. I closed my eyes and made a decision.

Did I jump? Or did I turn around?

How did it feel?

What did my classmates say to my?

# Story Starter 8

Willy looked like any other 5th grader. However, he had a secret that he had managed to keep since he was born. That is until his classmates George and Lily started to suspect there was something odd about him. He sometimes arrived at school barefoot, his hair was always messy, and he had extremely large teeth.

What ideas did George and Lily have that could explain Willy's strange behavior?

Did they ask Willy about it? Did he admit the truth or did he try to hide it?

Did they understand and keep the secret or was it time for the secret to be out in the open?

# ⋆ Story Starter 9 ⋆

When the engines started
failing halfway to Earth, the
captain decided to stop on the
moon so they could fix the
problem. Once there, the
astronauts put their suits on
and got out of the spaceship.
They were calm because they
had been trained to deal with
any kind of trouble, but they
didn't expect to find those
creatures.

What did the creatures look like?

Could the creatures talk? Or perhaps they communicated in another way?

Were they friendly? Or did they cause more problems

# Story Starter 10

Beth couldn't believe what she had found. She had heard the legend of Ed the pirate but she had never thought it was real. But there she was, holding an ancient treasure map that had his name on it.

What did Beth do with the map?

What was the legend of Ed the pirate?

Where did Ed hide the treasure?

# CHAPTER

2

# Fire up your IMAGINATION!

Getting started is perhaps the very hardest part about writing. But don't be scared of all that blank white space, it's all just a matter of unleashing your imagination and letting it run riot across the page! Even the most famous authors of best-selling books get struck by 'writer's block' once in a while, so you're certainly in good company if you're struggling to begin.

Everyone has an imagination, and you can bet there are millions of amazing ideas in there, just waiting to be let loose. Harnessing those ideas is a skill that you can easily learn, to take all those worlds, characters and fantastic storylines from within your mind, and put them down on paper.

**Here are some fun exercises to get your imagination sparked up and ready to go!**

*"Start writing, no matter what. The water does not flow until the faucet is turned on."*

*– Louis L'Amour (author)*

# EXERCISES

"The hardest thing about writing, for me, is facing the blank page."

- Octavia Spencer
(actress and author)

# 1. Write absolutely anything!

Get a blank piece of paper, pick up a pen, and write anything that comes into your head. It doesn't need to make sense; you can even make up words. Just let all those words flow from your mind and onto the paper. When the page is full, read it back. Does any of it make sense? Are there are ideas in there? This is a great way to get those thoughts out there. You never quite know what your own brain will come up with!

So grab a piece of paper and a pen, and set a timer for 3 minutes. Just keep writing, try not to stop to think, and keep going until the time is up. Then read what you've written and see if anything fires your imagination ready for a story!

# 2. Make a word soup page

So perhaps you have a vague idea about the type of story you'd like to write. You may want to write a story about dinosaurs, a romance, or an adventure set in space. Once you have one word, you can begin to gather more, and together, this 'word soup' will give you inspiration! So take your blank piece of paper and write down your starter word. Next, think of any words or phrases that come to mind when you picture the first word in your head. So for example, if your starter word is space, you may come up with more words such as rocket, laser beam, planet, aliens and suchlike. Then focus on these new words, and let your mind find even more related words and phrases, let your mind wander again. Perhaps the word alien conjures up an image of aliens that live underwater, or aliens that can read minds? Your word soup page can give you some great ideas to get started, but it's also handy to refer to when you're working on a story and want some extra inspiration. Getting started is perhaps the very hardest part about writing. But don't be scared of all that blank white space, it's all just a matter of unleashing your imagination and letting it run riot across the page! Even the most famous authors of best-selling books get struck by 'writer's block' once in a while, so you're certainly in good company if you're struggling to begin.

Everyone has an imagination, and you can bet there are millions of amazing ideas in there, just waiting to be let loose. Harnessing those ideas is a skill that you can easily learn, to take all those worlds, characters and fantastic storylines from within your mind, and put them down on paper.

**Here are some fun exercises to get your imagination sparked up and ready to go!**

*"For me, the blank page to draw on is a window to adventure."*

*- Eduardo Risso (comic artist)*

So now think of a starter word and write it on your piece of paper, and then write down as many words as you can that link to your first word.

## 3. The first words

When you're writing a new story, it can be tricky to get going with that very first line. But there are so many ways to start a story.

You could start with describing the main character so your readers can imagine them...

*"Ella was combing her long black hair, thinking how cool it would be if she was a witch"*

You could get right to the action with some dialogue...

*"'Run! Now!' yelled the mysterious stranger. 'Run for you life!'"*

You could set the scene by describing the location...

*"The snow had settled on the hilltops in the distance, but the sun was shining on the flelds as Marcus set out from the farmhouse to feed the sheep."*

Or how about starting with an intriguing question?

*"What would you do if one day you woke up and found you were living someone else's life?"*

These are just some of the many ways you could begin your story. Now can you come up with four more ways to get started?

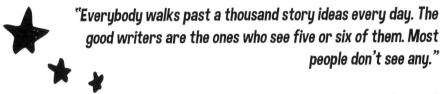

**"Everybody walks past a thousand story ideas every day. The good writers are the ones who see five or six of them. Most people don't see any."**

**- Orson Scott (author)**

## 4. Change a story you know well

Think about your favourite story from when you were little, a book you've recently read or a film that you've seen. Think about a major point in the story, a moment that changed everything. It could be when the hero outsmarted the villain, perhaps it's when the bank robbers get caught red-handed, or the moment a knight rescues a princess from an evil wizard. Now think about how you'd continue the story if these moments had happened differently. If that knight had been swallowed by a dragon before he had chance to rescue the princess, what would happen? Use your imagination to think of as many directions the story could go in. Perhaps the knight discovers that he can live inside the dragon so he takes control of the dragon's mind and turns him good. Maybe the princess decides not to bother waiting for a knight in shining armour and rescues herself, going on to be a powerful warrior. Perhaps the dragon was really an alien from the planet Wumbaloo and he takes the knight into deep space. It doesn't matter how far-fetched the story is, **because it's your story and so anything can happen!**

*"Never sit staring at a blank page or screen. If you find yourself stuck, write. Write about the scene you're trying to write. Writing about is easier than writing, and chances are, it will give you your way in."*

*- Laini Taylor (author)*

## 5. Discover another level of thinking

A good author will always question things, will always look deeper, and want to discover answers. One way to develop this skill is to question yourself. Taking a closer look at just what makes you the way you are. For instance, think about your favourite things, perhaps your favourite food, or your favourite place to visit. That's easy right? But then ask yourself, why are these things your favourite? Then you have to do a little more thinking. Why is pizza your favourite food? Is it because you love cheese? Perhaps it's the fun of sharing with the family? Or maybe it's a particular topping you enjoy? A place could bring back great memories, it may be that you love the activities you can do there such as playing on the beach, or something else? Think about why you do things, why you say things, and why others do and say the things they do. Understanding how people's minds work, including your own, is a great way to begin to develop characters in your stories that are realistic and have depth.

Here are some questions to answer yourself, then why not ask your friends and family too. It's amazing just how different human beings really are!

What's your favourite food and why?

Where is your favourite place in the world and why?

Who do you most like spending time with and why?

What's the best thing about school and why?

If a genie gave you one wish, what would it be and why?

So now you can look deeper into the characters in your story. If they're a spy, how did they become a spy? Perhaps their mother was a spy and passed on her skills? Maybe they went to spy school, or did they learn to be a spy in secret, reading books in bed after dark?
Pick one fact about each of your characters and create the backstory behind each fact.

# Tips

When faced with a blank page, here are some tips to kick start your creativity

**1**
Don't be afraid to just get started. No story was ever perfect to begin with. All the best authors write, re-write and re-write again. It's an ongoing process, so don't be worried about writing something that isn't that great to begin with. Get those ideas down and you can fine tune them later.

**2**
Don't let your writing stress you out. Writing should be fun, so if you're struggling, go and do something else for a while. You may well find that when you get back to your story, the ideas start to flood in!

**3**
Practice makes perfect, so try to write as often as you can. Every time you write, you're training your mind to be more and more creative. Even if it's only for a few minutes a day, it's a good habit to get into. Keeping a diary can be a great way to encourage yourself to keep writing on a daily basis.

**4**
If you have an idea but you're struggling to put it into words, try drawing your ideas. Once they're down on paper in any form, you won't forget that great idea, and the words will come to you later.

**5**
You don't need to know how the story ends. If you have an idea, but you have no idea how the story will end, that really shouldn't stop you from writing it. As you write the story, and the ideas and characters develop, an ending will often show itself to you of its own accord.

**6**
You also don't need to start at the beginning of the story. If you want to write the final big battle scene, then go ahead, you can fill in the backstory later. There is no law that says you have to write a story from the beginning to the end!

# Story Starters
## 11 - 20

# Story Starter 11

Beth tried to understand the instructions on the treasure map. First, she had to go to the city square and look for the obelisk. She geared up and was soon on her way. As she reached the monument, she opened the map again to see what she had to do next.

What was the set of instructions?

Did she find the treasure?

What did she do with it?

# Story Starter 12

I was walking through the jungle when I saw a beautiful, colorful toucan. As I reached for my camera, I felt something yanking it away from me. I looked up and saw a sneering monkey running away with it.

Why was I in the jungle?

Was there anyone else with me?

Did I chase the monkey and was I able to catch up with him?

# Story Star te r 13

Have you ever wondered why zebras have stripes? It's actually a funny story. One day a not-so-smart horse walked into a coal mine.

What made the zebra go into the mine?

How did the zebra get his stripes?

How did the horse get out of the mine and what happened when it returned home?

# Story Starter 14

Penny accidentally ran over Cassandra, the wickedest witch in her class, and in the process destroyed the alchemy project she was carrying. Unfortunately, Cassandra wasn't one to accept or understand apologies and immediately pulled out her wand.

Did Cassandra use her wand to put a spell on Penny?

How did Penny felt?

What happened to Penny and how did she react?

# ✧ Story Star te r 15

Gus stopped just before entering the corn maze and said "the first one out, wins". Melinda followed quickly and started wandering. Just as she thought she was reaching the exit, she found herself right in the middle again.

Did Melinda come up
with a way not to
get lost again

Did she managed to
get out at the end?

Who won the race?

# Story Star te r 16

Halloween was approaching and I couldn't wait to go trick or treating. My mom had promised me the most terrifying costume ever, but soon I realized we had different ideas of what scary meant. This costume was plain ridiculous. "I can't go out looking like this".

Story Starters 11-20

What did the
costume look like?

What costume did
I have in mind?

Did I manage to make
the costume more
scary at the end? Did I
get another costume?
Or did I wear the silly
costume anyway?

49

# Story Starter 17

Harry inherited his grandfather's time machine. He could go anywhere in time but had to follow two simple rules: 'Don't change a thing' and 'Never get caught'. He stepped eagerly into it and decided where he would go.

Out of all the places in time and space, where did Harry decide to go?

Who or what did he meet?

Did he break any rules? What were the consequences?

# ✦ Story Star te r 18 ✦

It all started with that mysterious note Fred found in his locker. "Meet me at the gym at lunchtime. Tell no one".

Who sent the note?

What did she or he want from Fred?

Did Fred tell anyone and that turned out to be for the best?

# Story Starter 19

I walked past the picture that hung in my school's auditorium every day. It was an old painting of the building. It took me a while to spot the human figure in the window of the principal's office. I took a closer look and that's when I realized that the figure was actually moving.

Who was the person in the picture?

How did the person get there?

Did I manage to communicate with the person in the picture?

# Story Starter 20

Anna woke up in the middle of the night. She was feeling thirsty so she went to the kitchen and opened the fridge door to get a drink. But when she looked inside, she saw a staircase! She rubbed her eyes thinking she was dreaming, but no, she was awake and the stairs were still there. So she decided to take a step forward.

What did Anna find downstairs?

Did she meet anyone?

How did she find her way back?

# CHAPTER

3

# BUILDING a Story

## (AND THE CHARACTERS IN IT)

So now you've been using your imagination, you probably have some ideas about the type of story you'd like to write. Maybe you can picture the setting for your story in your mind, or you have an idea for a cool hero and their great adventure. Once you have that seed of an idea, it's time to let it grow and see where the story will go!

Now isn't the time to worry about perfect spelling, or having everything in the right order, you don't even need to have names for your characters or places, you can work on all of that later. Now is the time to get those ideas down on paper and start to develop them.

**These exercises will help you to take your ideas and build them into a real story...**

# EXERCISES

"Imagination is more important than knowledge.
Knowledge is limited. Imagination encircles the world."

- Albert Einstein (scientist)

# 1. Creating a world

Every story has a setting, and so it's up to you to invent the world where your story takes place. When it comes to imagination, there are no limits, so you can do whatever you please – it's your story after all. So think about the type of setting you'd like for your story. Would you like an adventure set on a prehistoric island? A modern town? Or a planet in a distant galaxy?

Now you've chosen a setting, take a piece of paper and draw a map of it. Of course this can change later when the story grows and develops, but let you imagination run wild. If you're setting your story in a town, then mark the key places on your map. Choose a spot for the hero's house. If the hero is young, then perhaps the school will play a part, so mark that on the map. Maybe a name for the town and the school will spring into your mind. If they do, add them to your map.

Being able to see your new world like this can be very helpful when you're looking for more ideas for your story.

*"Laughter is timeless, imagination has no age and dreams are forever."*

*- Walt Disney (film producer)*

So now create a map with at least five important places marked on it.

# 2. Adding in the inhabitants of your world

Once you have a world, you need some characters to put into it. Now it's time to write a list of your main characters and a description of them. You may have a name in mind, or you can just write a description, the details can come later. Remember, you're making up the rules, so if your character is a talking dog or a green man from the planet Sneezle, that's all great stuff!

So write down one main character and a bit about them. Do they have a friend or helper? Write about them too. Is there an enemy they need to defeat? Add in at least two extra characters and see how you begin to picture them more clearly in your mind.

Here's an example:

> **Main character:** Jessica - Jessica is 12 years old, she lives with her parents and has a secret power nobody knows about except her best friend.
> **Best friend:** Jessica's best friend is also 12 years old, they go to school together. Her name is Emma and she lives nearby.
> **Enemy:** Jessica's enemy is a witch called Wendy. The witch is very powerful and wants to be the only person in the world with special powers.

**"Bring ideas in and entertain them royally, for one of them may be the king."**

**- Mark Van Doren (poet)**

Now is your turn. **Think about your main character...**

What is their name?
How old are they?
What do they do? Do they go to school? Do they have a job?
Where do they live?
Do they have any special skills or powers?

**Describe their personality**

Are they shy? Adventurous? Bossy?
Who are their closest friends?
Who are their enemies?

# 3. What is the point of the story?

There may be lots of twists and turns along the way, but a story will have a main point, a focus, a goal. Think about your characters. What is the storyline going to be? In our example in exercise 2, it could be that Wendy the witch tries to steal Jessica's powers. So she needs to find a way to keep her powers. Now this is where it gets interesting. What would Jessica's ultimate goal be? There are many options. She could kill the witch, she could find a more powerful witch to banish Wendy to another world, she could increase her own powers to defeat the witch, or she could make friends with the witch and persuade her that it's okay for everyone to have their own special powers. Wouldn't that be a fun way to end the story?
Here's another example for you...

- The main character Simon is lost in space and he needs to get home. How will he get there?

- He could get a job on a spaceship that will eventually visit Earth.

- He could pretend he is a famous Earth prince and offer a large reward to anyone who takes him home.

- He could hitch-hike his way home, grabbing a series of short lifts across the galaxy.

- He could seek out a race of magical beings who can open portals to other galaxies.

- He could stow away on a spaceship, hoping it's headed in the right direction.

*"Be yourself. Above all, let who you are, what you are, what you believe, shine through every sentence you write, every piece you finish."*

**- John Jakes (author)**

Now you give it a go!
Think about the beginning of your story, and come up with at least five different ways in which it could end.

## 4. What will happen along the way?

Most stories would be quite boring if they simply had a beginning and an end, no matter how exciting the subject. The beginning sets the scene, the end wraps everything up, but it's in the middle where the adventure takes place and the real magic happens.
Check out this terrible story...

*Eric's dad was a famous archaeologist. He discovered a priceless ancient relic, but one night it vanished from the dig site, and mysterious footprints led away from the area. Eric decided to set off on a quest to find the relic. The next day he tracked it down and brought it back, everyone was very happy.*

You see, that could be a great story, but you need to hear about the journey to really appreciate the happy ending. So once you have the idea for a story, jot down some ideas for what might happen in the middle. You don't have to use all the ideas, but having them down on paper will give you inspiration.

Let's take Eric's quest as an example. Here are some ideas for what could happen to him...

- The footprints could be bird tracks, a bird could have taken the relic to its nest.

- Eric could get the relic back, but then be kidnapped by bandits trying to steal the relic.

- Eric could be bewitched into forgetting his quest, and only remember it when he's kissed by a princess.

- He could find that the relic has been hidden with another 1000 relics that all look the same and he needs to discover which is the true one.

So now write down some ideas for the magical middle part of your story.

- Will your hero travel? If so where?

- Will they meet other people along the way – who?

- Will there be a battle or fight?

- Will they get lost?

- Will they save someone or need to be rescued themselves?

- Will they make friends, or enemies or fall in love?

# Tips

**1.**
Keep notes of your setting and each character. As your story develops, so will the places and people in it. So when you decide that your main character wears glasses, and the town you've set the story in is by the sea, write down all these details and keep re-reading them so it all becomes more real to you. If you believe in your characters then your readers will too!

**2**
Don't be scared to go wild with your story. You make the rules, so if you want to have your main character be turned into a frog or the town they live in be transported to the other side of the world, then go with it.

**3.**
If you're setting your story in another place or time, then it's a good idea to learn more about it to make it seem realistic. So, if your story takes place in Australia, Ancient Egypt, or a prehistoric jungle, learn more about these places and you'll pick up some details you can use in your stories.

**4.**
Your characters don't have to be perfect. Think about it, no one is really perfect so it can make the people in your story seem more real if they have flaws. A super hero with a fear of spiders, a king who really hates wearing a crown, a teacher who doesn't like children, a boy who saves the planet but he never gets round to tidying his bedroom.

**5.**
Keep a small notebook with you all the time, or make notes on a mobile phone if you have one. You never know when inspiration might hit for a plot idea or a character's name. Write it down quick before you forget!

# Story Starters

## 21 - 30

# STORY STARTER 21

My grandma had a hobby. She liked collecting garden gnomes. She had over twenty placed around her lawn because she insisted that they protected her home. One afternoon, I came by her house unannounced and when I opened the front door, I saw that these miniature figures were doing her housework.

Did I ask my grandma what on earth was going on? if so, what did she say?

Where did she get these gnomes?

What else could the gnomes do?

# STORY STARTER 22

As he was walking by the zoo's savannah exhibit, someone hissed. He looked around and saw no one. He started walking again when he heard "Hey, boy, come here and give me a hand, will you?", but this time he saw where the voice came from. A meerkat was looking at him while trying to reach a bag of peas.

Was it the first time he had talk to an animal?

Could he understand the other animals too?

Did the boy helped the meerkat?

# STORY STARTER 23

His neighbor, Mrs. Gilmore, gave him the creeps. She looked like a nice old lady, but he knew that she was hiding something. One night as he was taking out the trash, he saw that the door was open, so he decided to take a look inside. As he stepped inside Mrs. Gilmore's home, the door shut behind him. "Oh dear, you shouldn't have done that".

What was
Unsettling inside of
Mrs. Gilmore house?

What was Mrs.
Gilmore's story?

Did he escape from Mrs.
Gilmore house? How?

# STORY STARTER 24

My mom was going to kill me. It was an accident, but I wasn't so sure she would see it that way. In a series of unfortunate events, I dropped my birthday cake, the one she had spent all night baking, onto the floor, and now I had two hours before she got back from work to fix it.

How did I decide to fix the problem?

Did mom find out what I did? Or did I get away with it?

What else happened on my birthday?

# STORY STARTER 25

Abigail woke up, yawned and stretched and got out of bed. Another boring school day. She opened her curtains to check the weather. Her walk to school was always worse when it was raining. It wasn't raining outside, because there was no outside! All she could see was total blackness, dotted with stars. No streetlights, no lights from windows across the street. Where was she? She shouted for her mum and dad, but got no reply. Slowly, she opened her bedroom door, determined to find out what was going on.

Where was Abigail? Was she even in her house or was it an illusion?

Where were her parents?

Why had this happened?

# STORY STARTER 26

Ty was set on winning the neighborhood's annual Christmas decorations contest. He had been planning for weeks where to put each of the Christmas figures, ornaments, garlands and lights. That Saturday morning, he went to the cellar to look for the decoration boxes and with horror discovered that they were all damp and ruined.

Why was Ty so desperate to win the contest?

Did Ty come up with a new plan?

How had the decorations become ruined? Did someone do it on purpose to stop him for winning?

# STORY STARTER 27

Ginny was walking home from school when she found a stuffed toy on the sidewalk. It was an old and grubby yellow duck. She took a closer look and saw it had a name written on the label "Oli Hamlin". She wasn't sure why, but she picked it up and decided on the spot that she would find its owner.

What steps did Ginny take to find the owner?

Did she find Oli?

Was she rewarded?

# STORY STARTER 28

You might know my parents. My dad is the fastest man alive, and my mom is known for her heat vision. You might think that I would have inherited their cool powers, but instead, all I got was super-stretching fingers. That is, the ability to make my fingers grow three feet long.

What funny situations did my fingers get me into?

Did my super stretchy fingers ever become useful?

Did I ever team up with my parents to use all our skills together?

# STORY STARTER 29

An egg appeared in Mika's backyard. He thought that it might have fallen from a nest in the tree, but unable to find its mother, he took it in and set up a home-made incubator. Three days later the egg began to hatch and what emerged from inside was no ordinary bird. It had horns, four legs, and suddenly a small puff of fire escaped from its mouth.

What exactly was it that hatchet from the egg?

Did Mika decide to keep the baby?

What happened when it grew up?

# STORY STARTER 30

The moment I rubbed the oil lamp, a genie appeared before me. Without any introductions he said, "I'll grant you one wish, but be wise". I didn't hesitate and answered, "I wish I could fly". With a flick of his fingers, I got what I wanted. But not the way I had pictured it. Suddenly, two large wings started growing on my back and began flapping.

What happened next?

Where did I go?

Did I keep the wings forever?

# CHAPTER

4

# Making your STORY the Best it Can be

Once you've written your story, take some time to sit back and feel proud of it. You've written a story, and that's pretty amazing! But why not do what professional authors do, and make it even better? Read your story through and think about the storyline, the characters, is there anything missing? Does something need explaining a little better?

With a dictionary to hand, check your spelling and grammar. Now is the time to fine tune all the details and make that good story, a really great story!

**Here are some exercises that you can use to make your story even more brilliant.**

# EXERCISES

"If there's a book that you want to read, but it hasn't been written yet, then you must write it."

- Toni Morrison (author)

# 1. Let other people read your story

A great way to make your story better is to find out what other people think of it. So ask your friends and family to have a read through and let you know what they felt were the best parts, if they thought anything was missing or was rushed. Did they like the characters? Could they imagine the places in the story? Did they feel happy and sad along with the story? A really good story makes people feel as if it's true, you're almost there with the characters, experiencing the adventure. If a book makes you excited, scared or even makes you cry, then it's done the job the author wanted.

So write out some questions to ask your new readers and use their answers to make your story even better! Here are some ideas...

*What was your favourite part of the story?*

*Were any parts of the story boring?*

*Who was your favourite character and why?*

*Is there anything else you'd like to have happened in the story?*

**"I kept always two books in my pocket, one to read, one to write in."**

**- Robert Louis Stevenson (author & poet)**

Can you come up with five more questions to ask?

# 2. Tell yourself your story!

When you're reading your own written words, it can be hard to spot mistakes. A fun way to help you spot errors is to read your story out loud. It's even better if you record yourself reading it so you can play it back as often as you want.

1. First read your story out loud and whenever you come across an error, make a note. On this read through you might well spot some spelling and grammar problems.

2. Correct these first errors, and read your story again, this time, recording it.

3. Now play your recording and try to forget that it's your story. Imagine you're listening to this story for the first time. You'll not only pick up on grammar errors, but you might also get some ideas for parts of your story you'd like to make longer, more suspenseful or more scary. You might feel that some people or places are not described clearly enough, or perhaps you just want the story to go on longer.

> **"Write the kind of story you would like to read. People will give you all sorts of advice about writing, but if you are not writing something you like, no one else will like it either."**
>
> **- Meg Cabot (author)**

## 3. Find some new words

When you're reading back through your story, have you noticed that you're using the same words over and over again? It's good to mix it up a bit to stop things getting repetitive, so have a go at finding some different ways to say the same thing. For example, if you find you describe something as 'cool' a lot, then how about swapping some out for alternatives such as 'awesome' 'amazing' 'fabulous' or 'terrific'? If you use the word 'scary' a lot, then consider using 'terrifying' 'creepy' or 'eerie'.

So now go through your story and underline words that you've used too often. Make a list of these words and search for some good alternatives on www.thesaurus.com. You'll find plenty of different options to use so swap out some of the repeated words for your new words. Knowing lots of words is a great skill for any budding author!

> **"If you want to be a writer, you must do two things above all others: read a lot and write a lot."**
>
> **- Stephen King (author)**

## 4. Make it a real book with some fun extras

Take a look at your own bookshelves and you'll see that you're missing a few things that will really make your story into a real book. Here are some ideas for extra content, why not give them all a go?

**Illustrations** - Pictures in a book really help the reader to imagine the characters and the settings. You could draw your own illustrations, or why not ask an artistic friend to contribute to your book? Just don't forget to give them credit!

**A great title and a front cover** - They say you shouldn't judge a book by its cover, but it really helps for your book to actually have a cover, and of course, the main thing on the front cover will be the title of the book. If you haven't come up with a title yet, now is the time to do so! The cover will also need your name on it, you can make it as large as you like, it's your book after all!

**About the author** - Here's your chance to write a little bit about yourself, your life and why you love writing stories!
A thanks and dedication page – It's nice to say thank you to anyone who has helped you with editing your book, been an inspiration, or simply given you encouragement with your story writing.

# Tips

**1**

A notepad and pen is ideal for making notes and jotting down ideas, but when it comes to writing your story, it's best to work on a computer so you can easily make changes. All the best stories go through lots of revisions, so be prepared to alter your story several times as you come up with better and better ideas!

**2**

Don't forget to back up your writing. Have a USB stick to hand to regularly copy your work onto. It would be awful to lose all that hard work!

**3**

When you're reading back through your story, look for things that are out of place for the setting. For example, you don't want your character to be checking Instagram if your story is set before it was even invented. Doing extra research to make the details believable will really enhance your story.

**4**

Don't be in a rush to finish. Getting to the end of a story is exciting. You'll be keen to print it out and proudly present it to your friends and family, but take your time. Read through it, check for errors, then put it aside and come back to it again another day. It's amazing what you spot with fresh eyes.

**5**

Keep making notes. Your book may be completed, but is the story finished? Are the characters still lurking in your mind, perhaps ready for more adventures? If you have an idea, write it down, then one day you may have enough ideas ready for a sequel!

# Story Starters
## 31 - 40

# STORY STARTER 31

Kyle rubbed his eyes in disbelief. Was that a squirrel wearing a tutu? He decided to follow the animal through the woods and discovered the most unbelievable scene.

What did he find?

Were there other animals in clothing?

What was the occasion?

# STORY STARTER 32

Can you believe I ran over the Easter Bunny? I was riding my bike when I felt a bump under my wheels. I immediately turned around and saw a basket lying on the ground, and a few feet away, a rabbit clutching its leg. As I came to its aid, I heard a high-pitched voice say, "Oh no, who's going to hide the eggs now?".

Did I offer my help?

How did the Easter Bunny feel and react?

Did I hide the eggs for the bunny?

# STORY STARTER 33

Isa was reading a book at the beach when she saw a bottle floating to the shore. She quickly ran to it and picked it up, only to discover a note inside. It was a YouTube video url. She was intrigued so she grabbed her smartphone and typed in the address. "Hello, Isa. I'm you, from the future".

How old was the woman from the video?

What did she say?

Did Isa from the future give any advice? or ask Isa to do something?

# STORY STARTER 34

It was her parents' anniversary and Molly wanted to treat them with a nice dinner. She went into the kitchen and started preparing the one dish she had learned from her aunt, spaghetti with meatballs. It was only after her parents had eaten their meal that she realized she had made a mistake. She had accidentally used her mother's secret ingredient. The jar of herbs she had been strictly told to never ever use.

What did the secret ingredients do to the parents?

Did Molly tell her parents what happened?

How did the evening end?

# STORY STARTER 35

That morning I woke up, brushed my teeth and went down to have breakfast. It was just like any other morning, that is until my mom asked me how I was and I burst into song. I tried to stop, but immediately I realized that I couldn't.

What song(s) did I sing?

Did my mom belive me that I couldn't stop?

Did I manage to get my voice back? How? Did it wear off? Did I need medice? Was there someone who could cure me?

# STORY STARTER 36

Jess was on a mission to blow the biggest bubble gum bubble in history. She opened each piece one by one and proceeded to put each one in her mouth. When she reached fifty, she started chewing and blowing. At first it was tricky, but soon an enormous bubble came out of her mouth, and suddenly she started to float above the ground.

How far did Jess float?

How did she managed to get back on the ground?

What happened when she got back?

# STORY STARTER 37

Tom and Mark were identical twins. And yes, they used to switch places all the time. Mark would take Tom's math quizzes and Tom would take over his brother's spot in P.E. classes. They usually got away with it until the school principal realized Tom had a small scar over his left brow.

Did the brothers get caught after the principal noticed the scar?

Did they manage to outwit the principal?

Could anyone else tell the twins appart?

# STORY STARTER 38

Billy, the penguin had captivated the world with his dancing. He went viral overnight and was invited onto every TV talk show. As soon as he got into town, he realized he didn't own any proper clothing.

What type of clothing was he looking for? Did he find anything his size?

What happened on the talk shows?

What did his future hold?

# STORY STARTER 39

Minnie had a weird fascination with supermarkets. She loved roaming through the aisles, seeing the different displays, and picking free food from the sample stations. Her ultimate dream was to spend a night inside a store, so one Friday evening while doing some last-minute shopping she decided to hide in the bathroom until the supermarket was closed.

What was it like when she left the bathroom?

Did she felt scared and lonely, or did she have an amazing time?

What did she do in the supermarket?

# STORY STARTER 40

Yuri was determined to reach the other end of the rainbow. He had heard stories of pots of gold guarded by leprechauns, but he was set on finding the truth. So he patiently waited for a rainy day and as soon as the first sunlight hit the water droplets and the rainbow was visible, he embarked on his quest.

Where did he start
the journey?

Was somebody with
him?

What did he find at
the end of the
rainbow?

Printed in Great Britain
by Amazon

20406951R00066